Jour ‡ la plage

plage

Coloriage

Coloring Pages for Kids

Coloring Pages for Kids
An imprint of Ciparum LLC

Jour ‡ la plage Coloriage
© 2017 Ciparum LLC
All rights reserved.
ISBN-10:1-63589-395-X
ISBN-13:978-1-63589-395-3

Coloring Pages for Kids

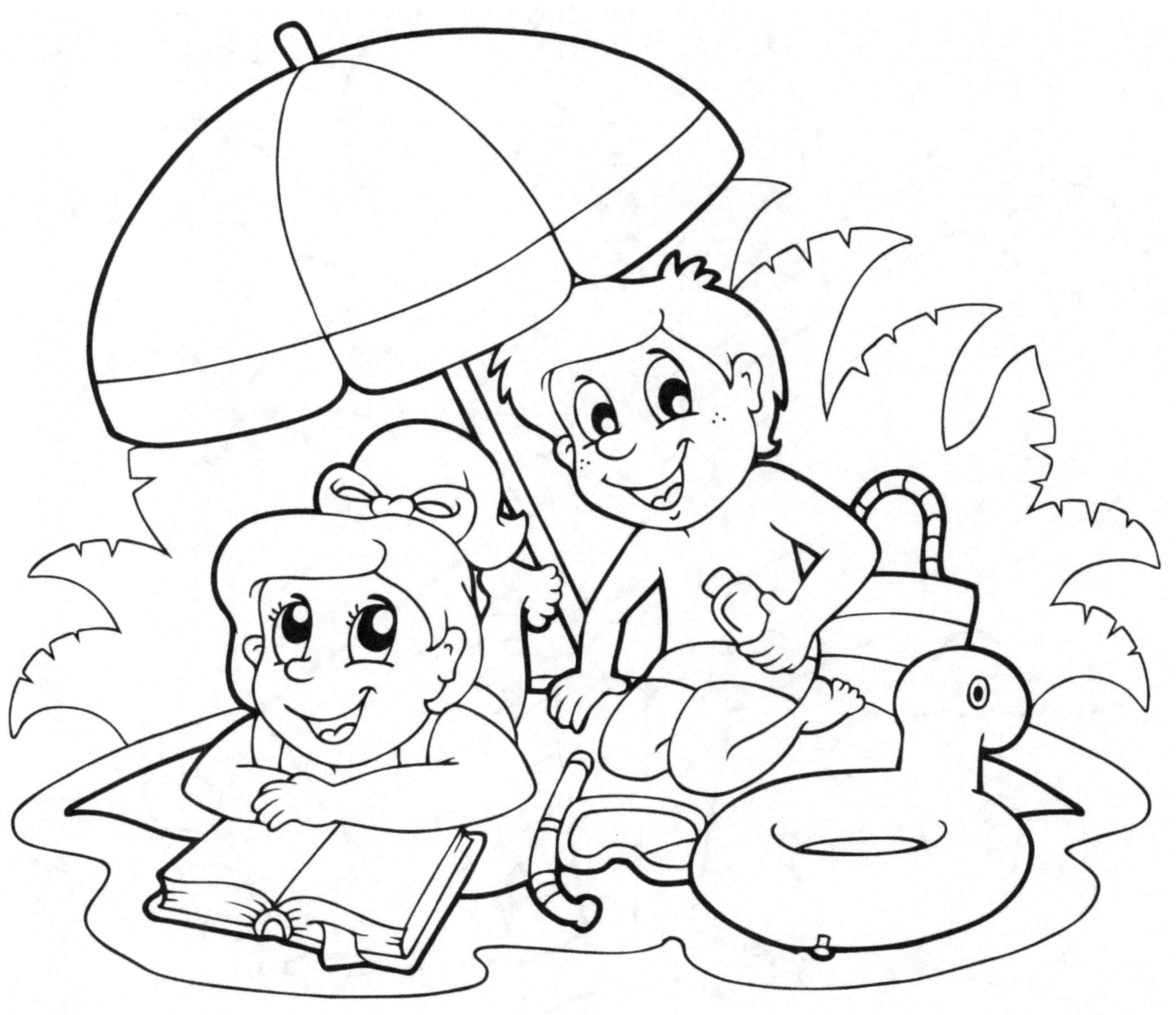

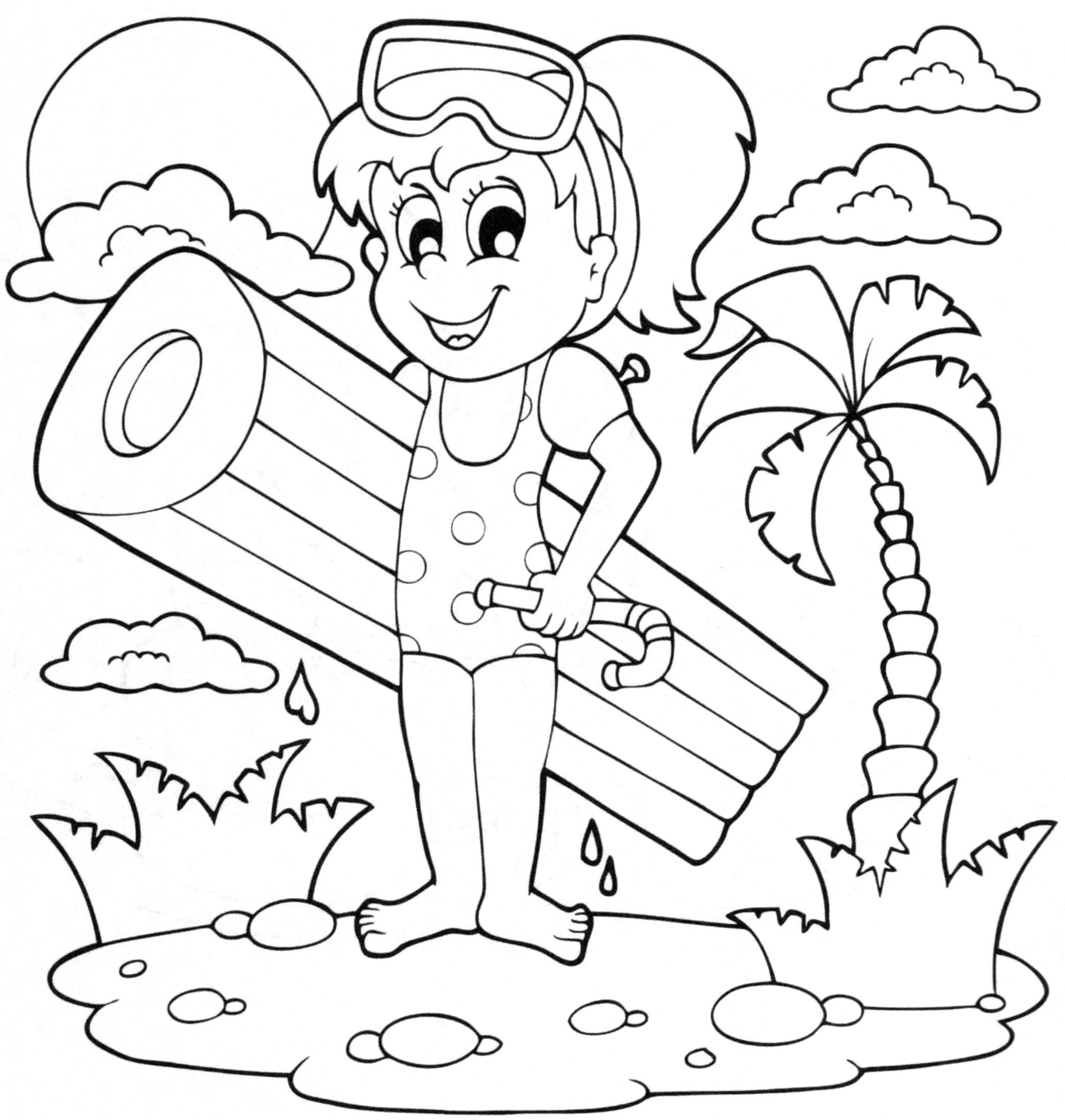

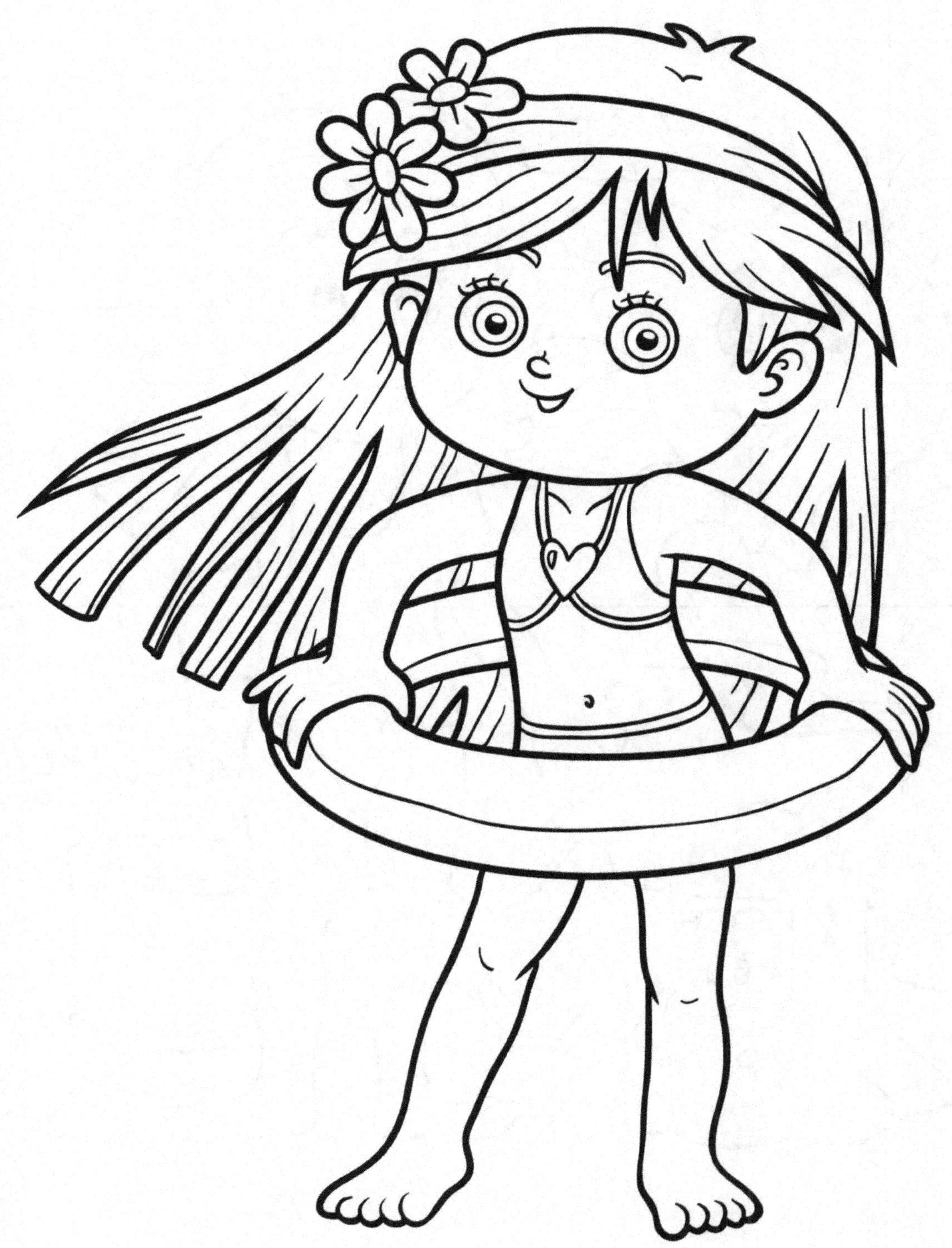

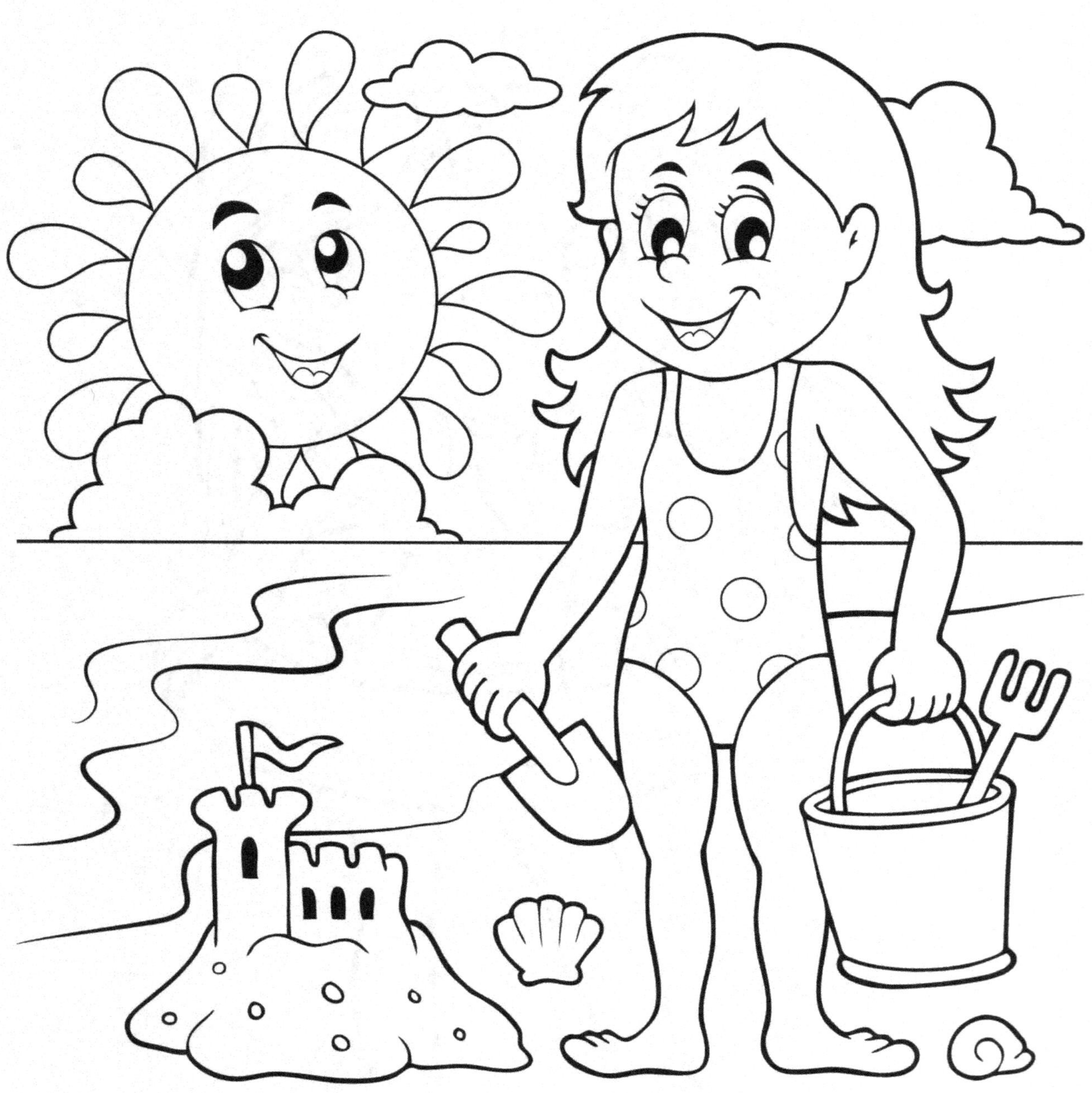

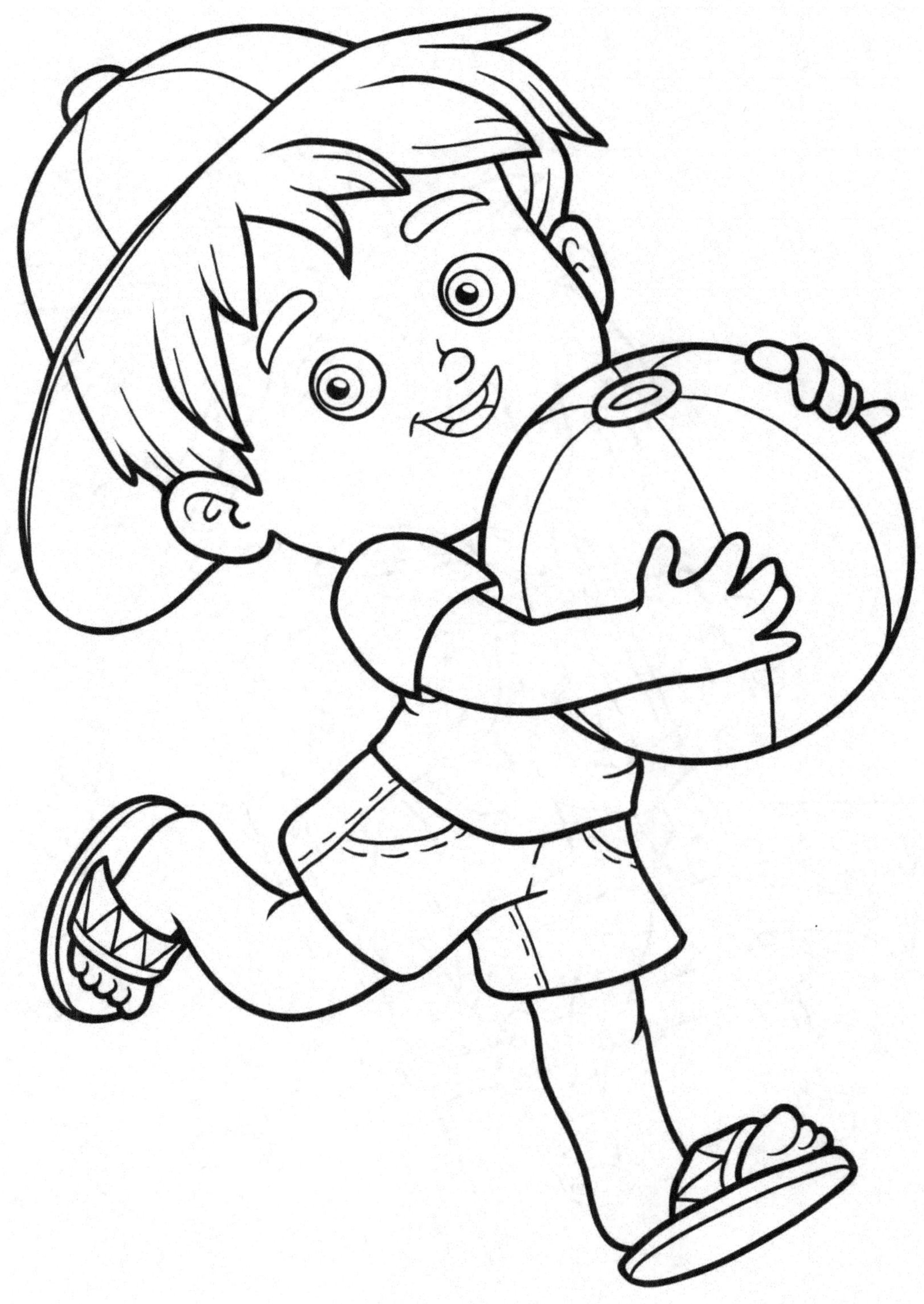

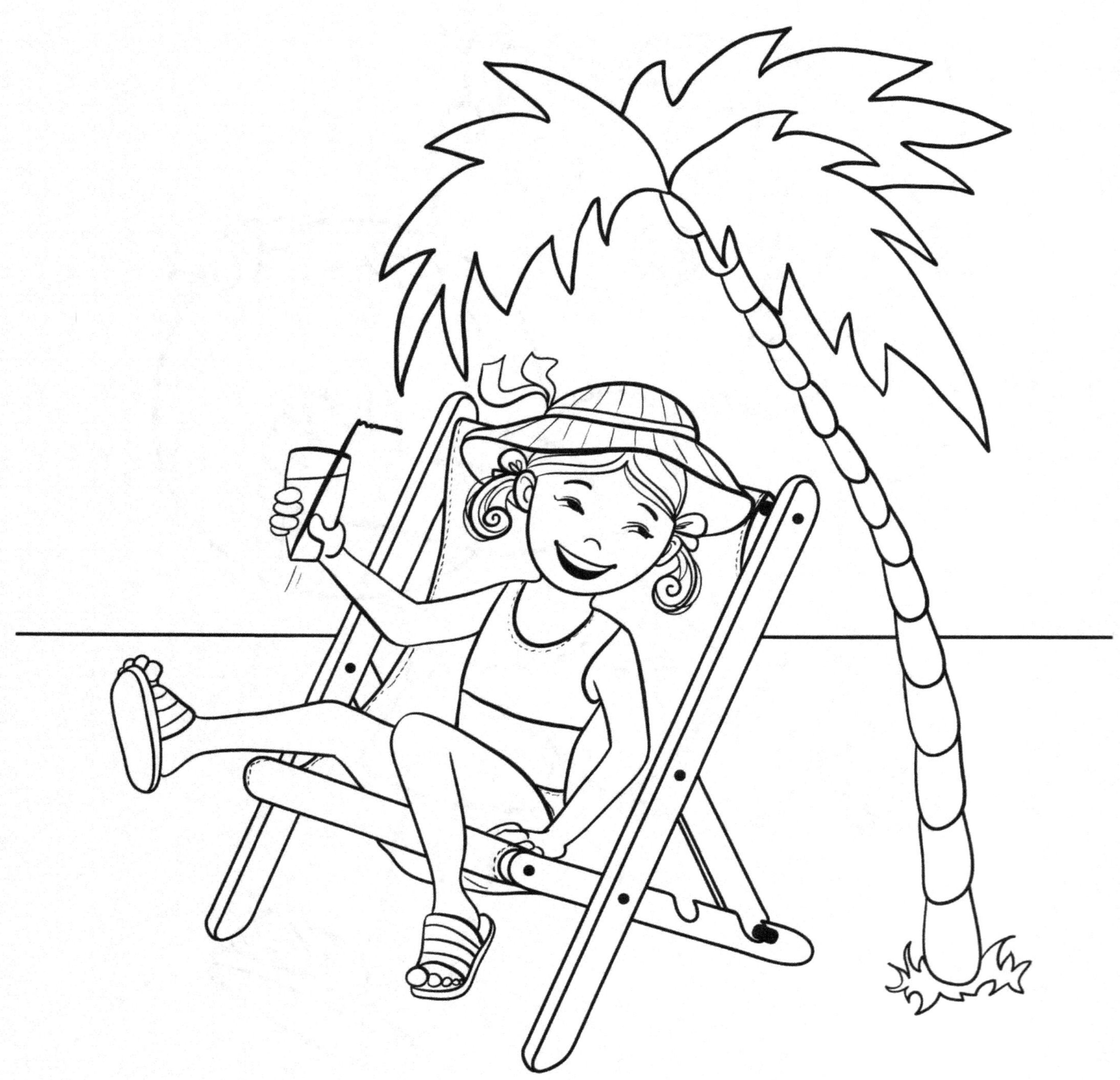

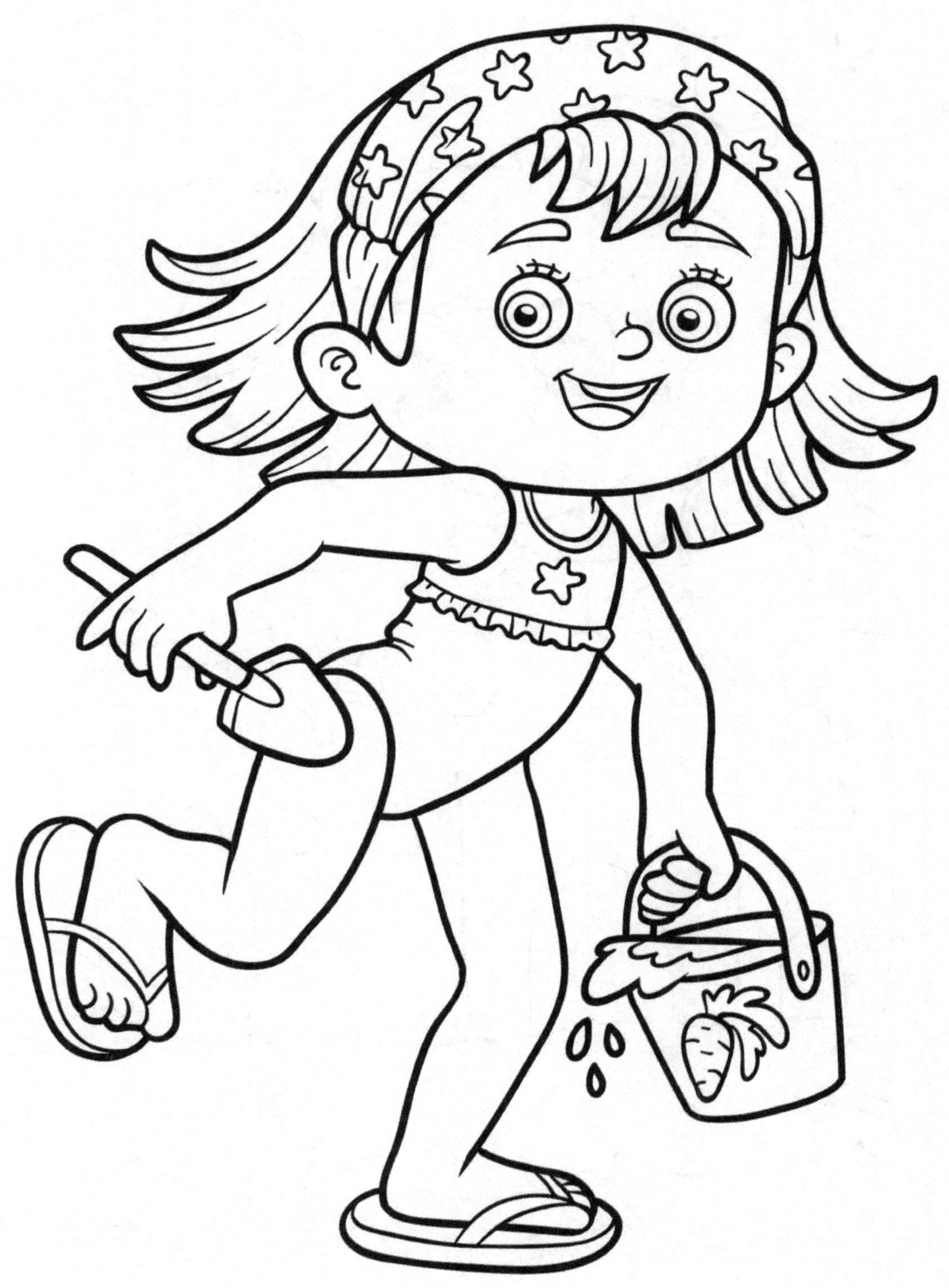

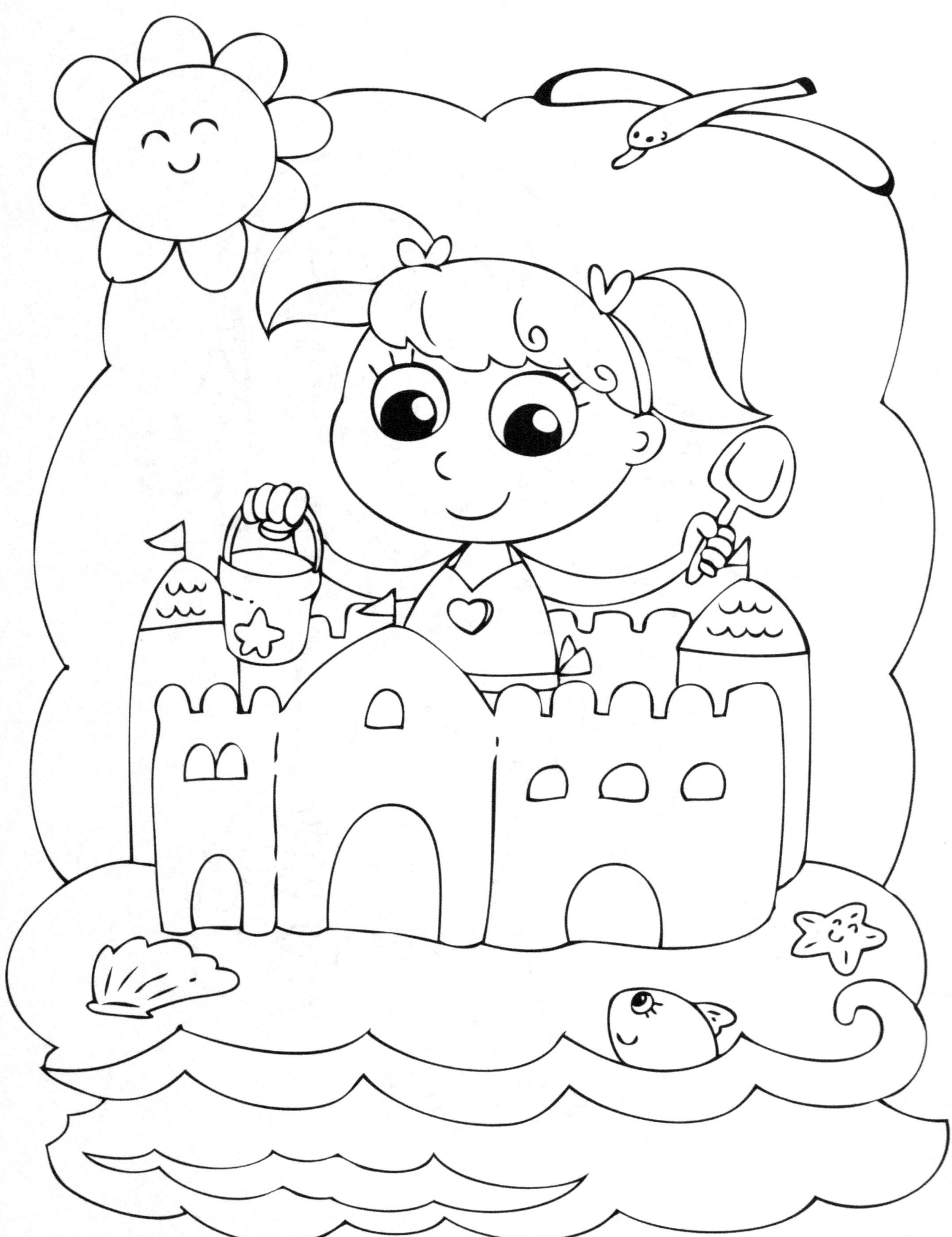

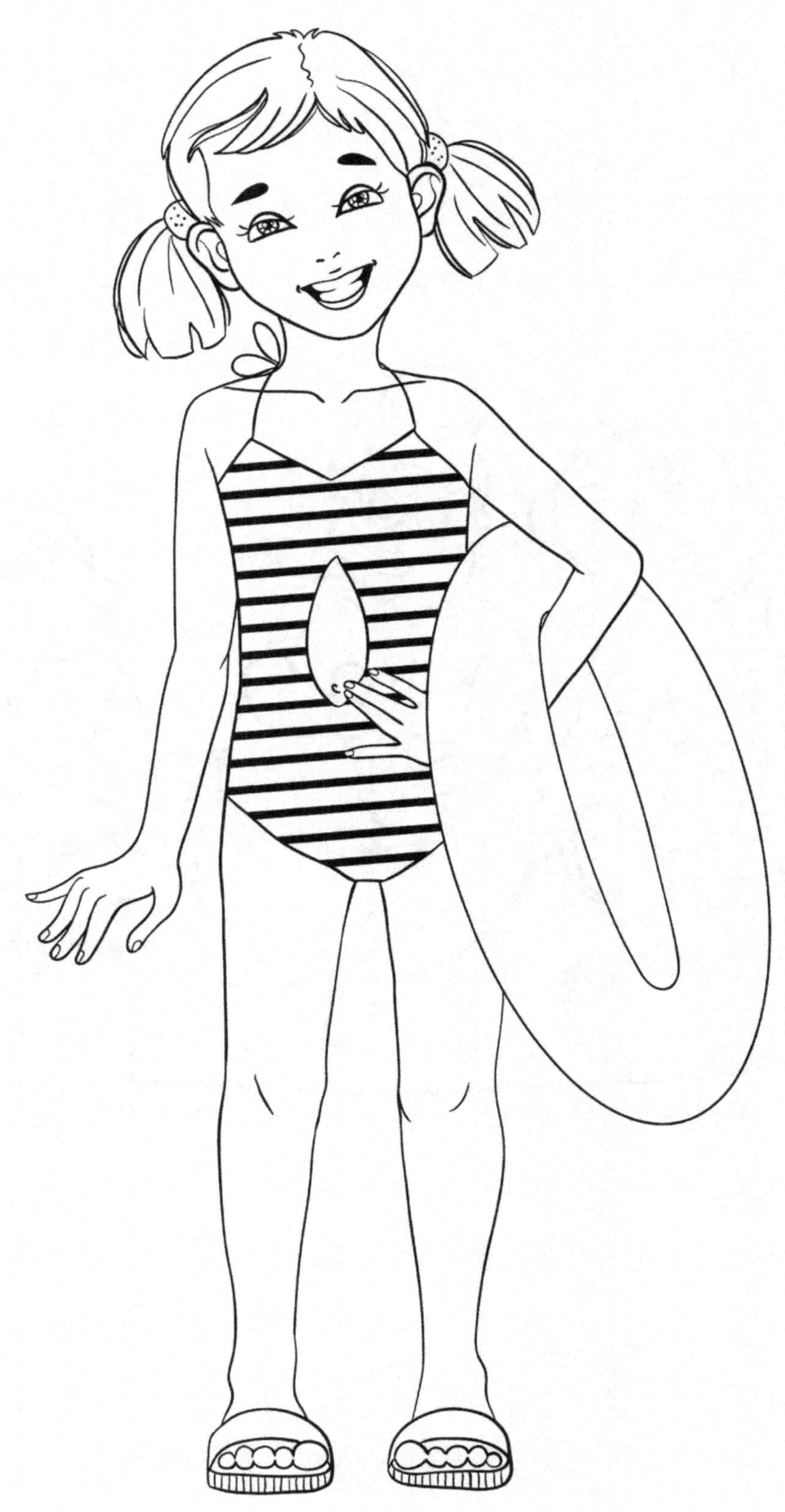

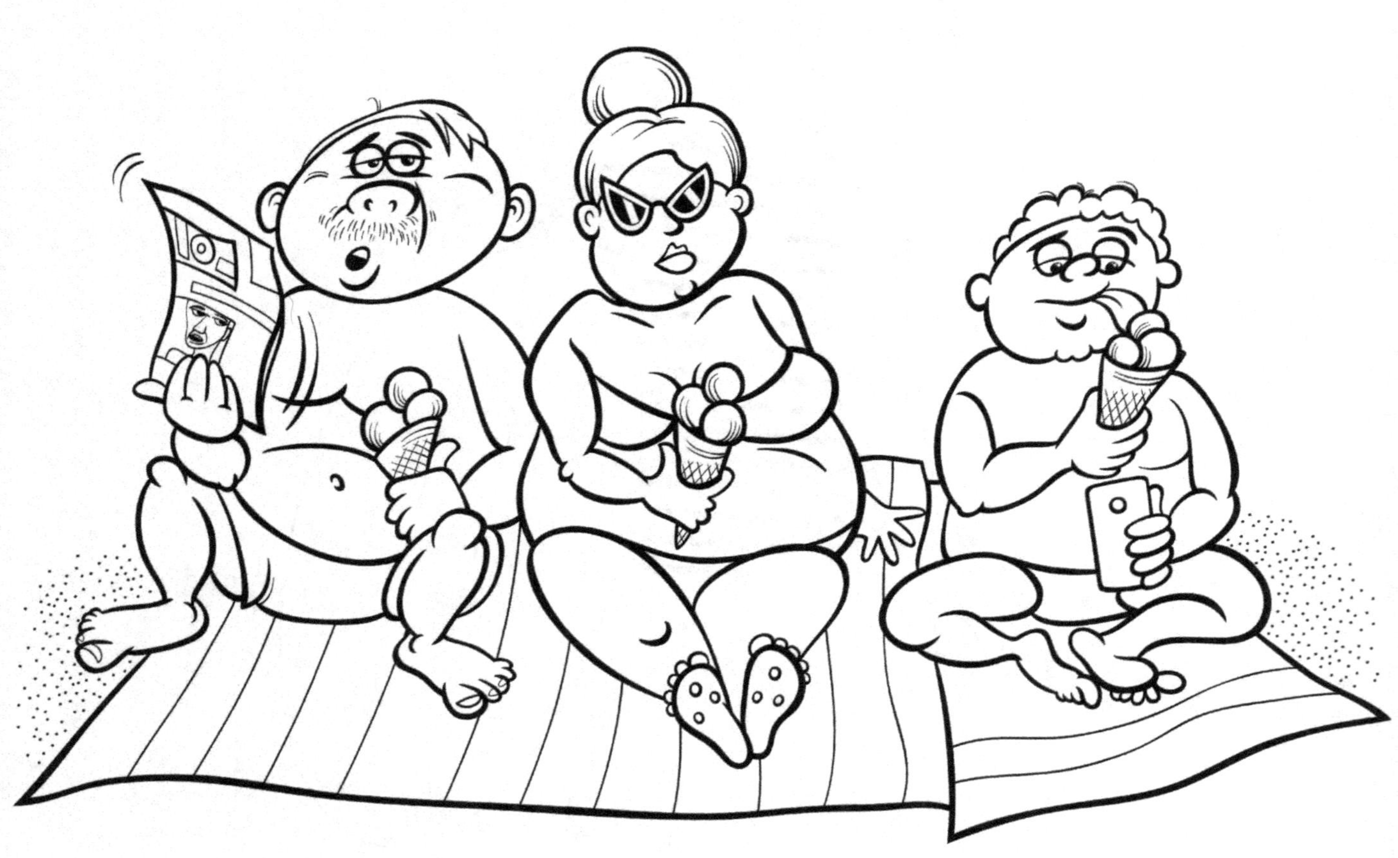

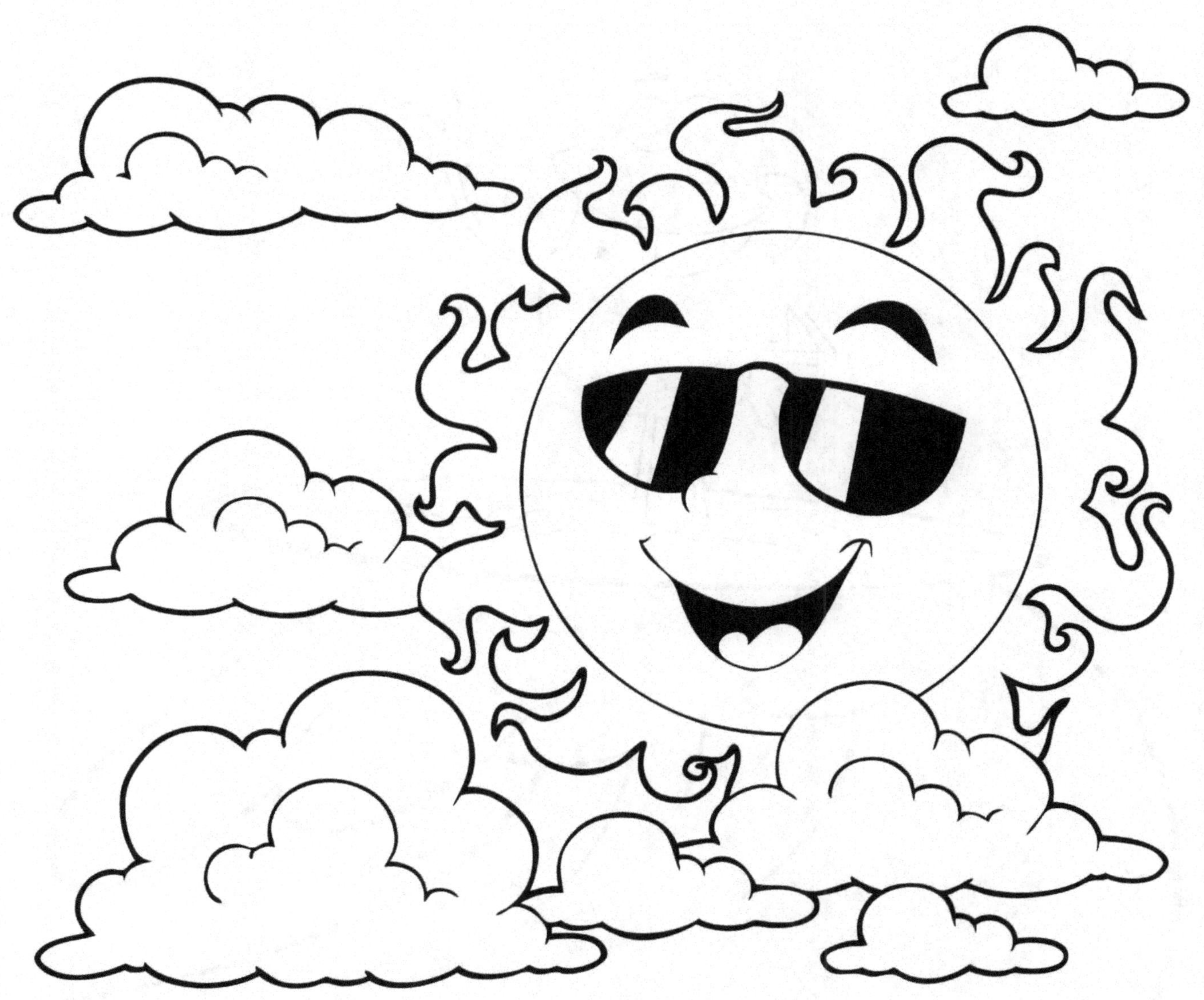

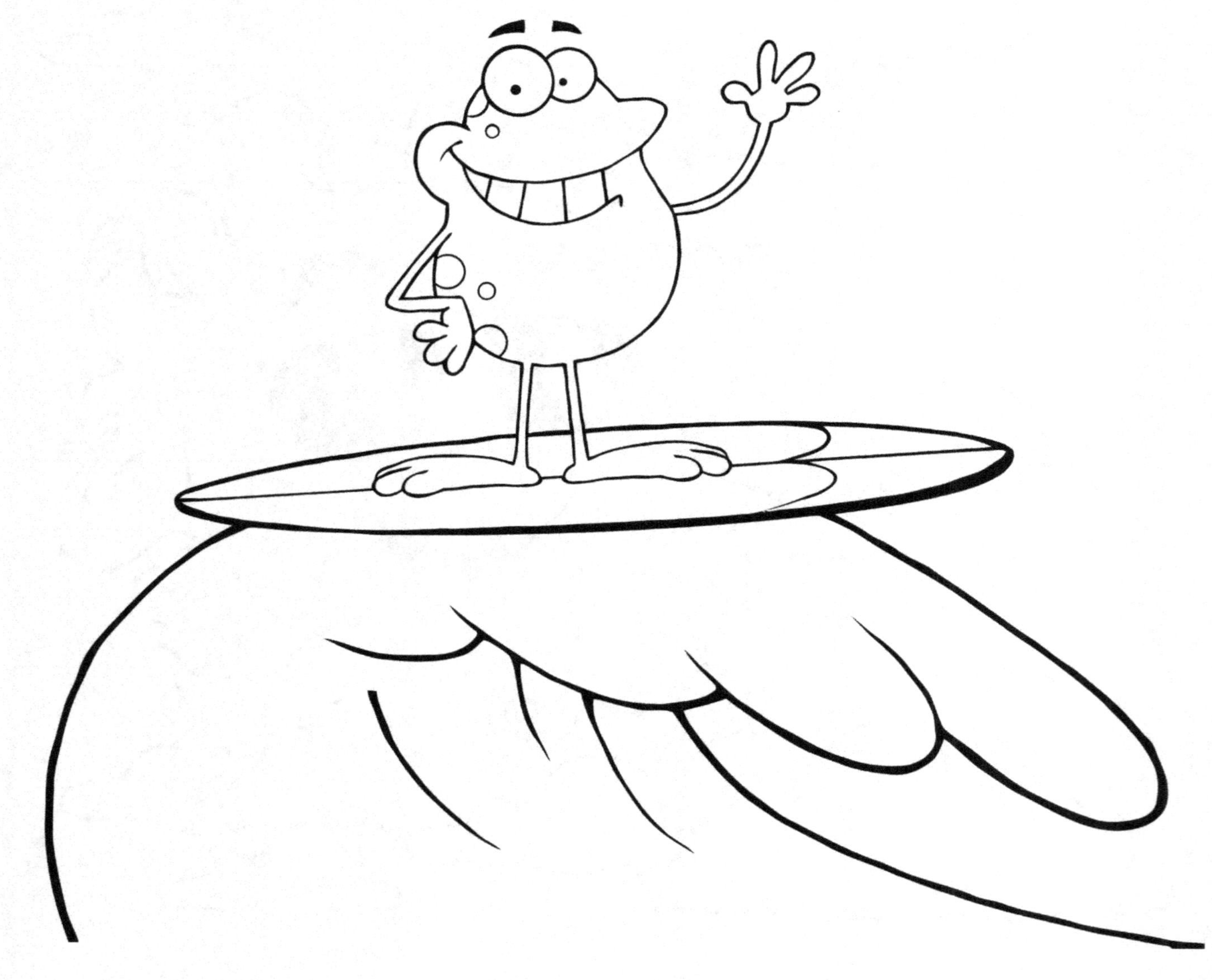

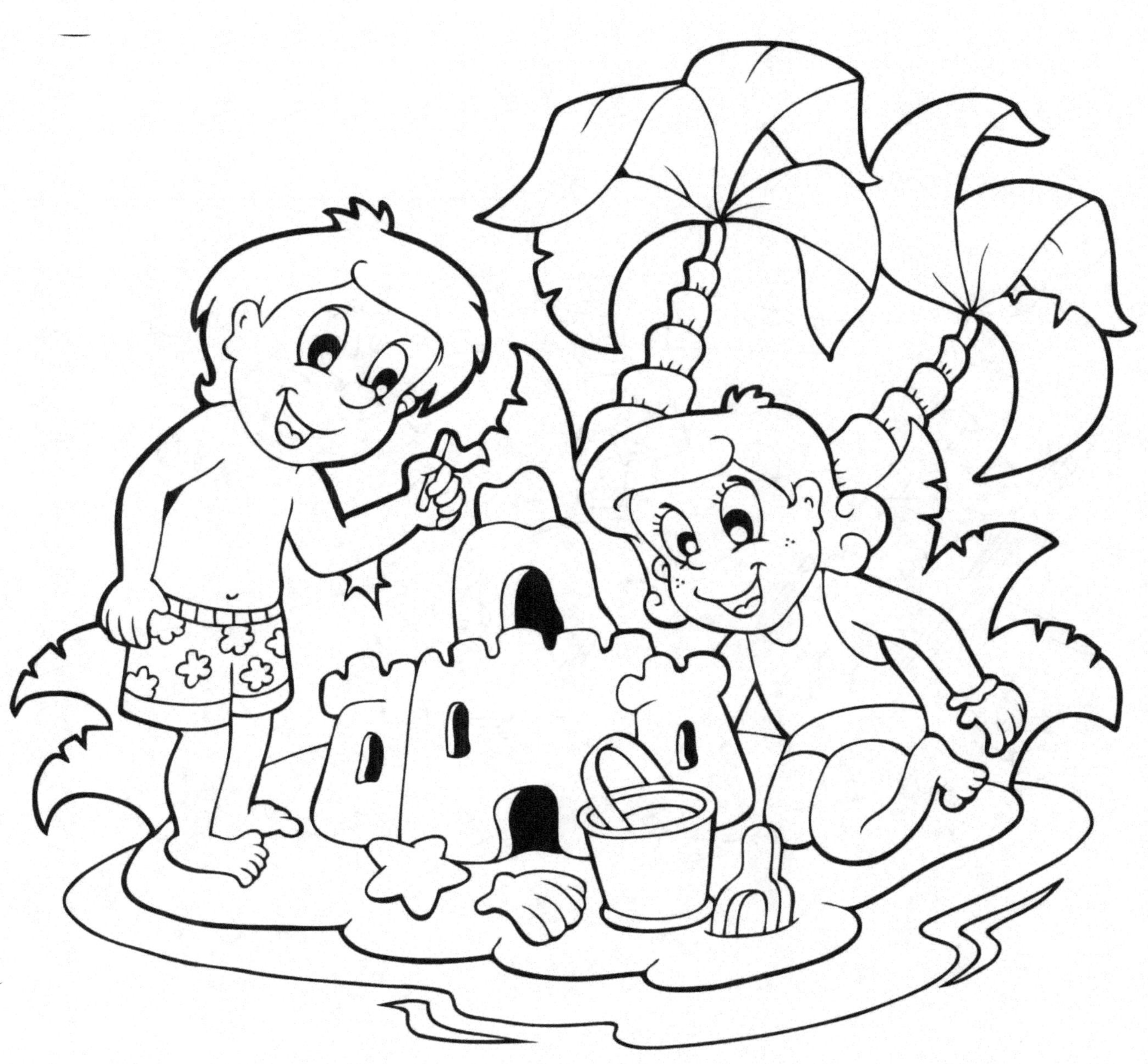

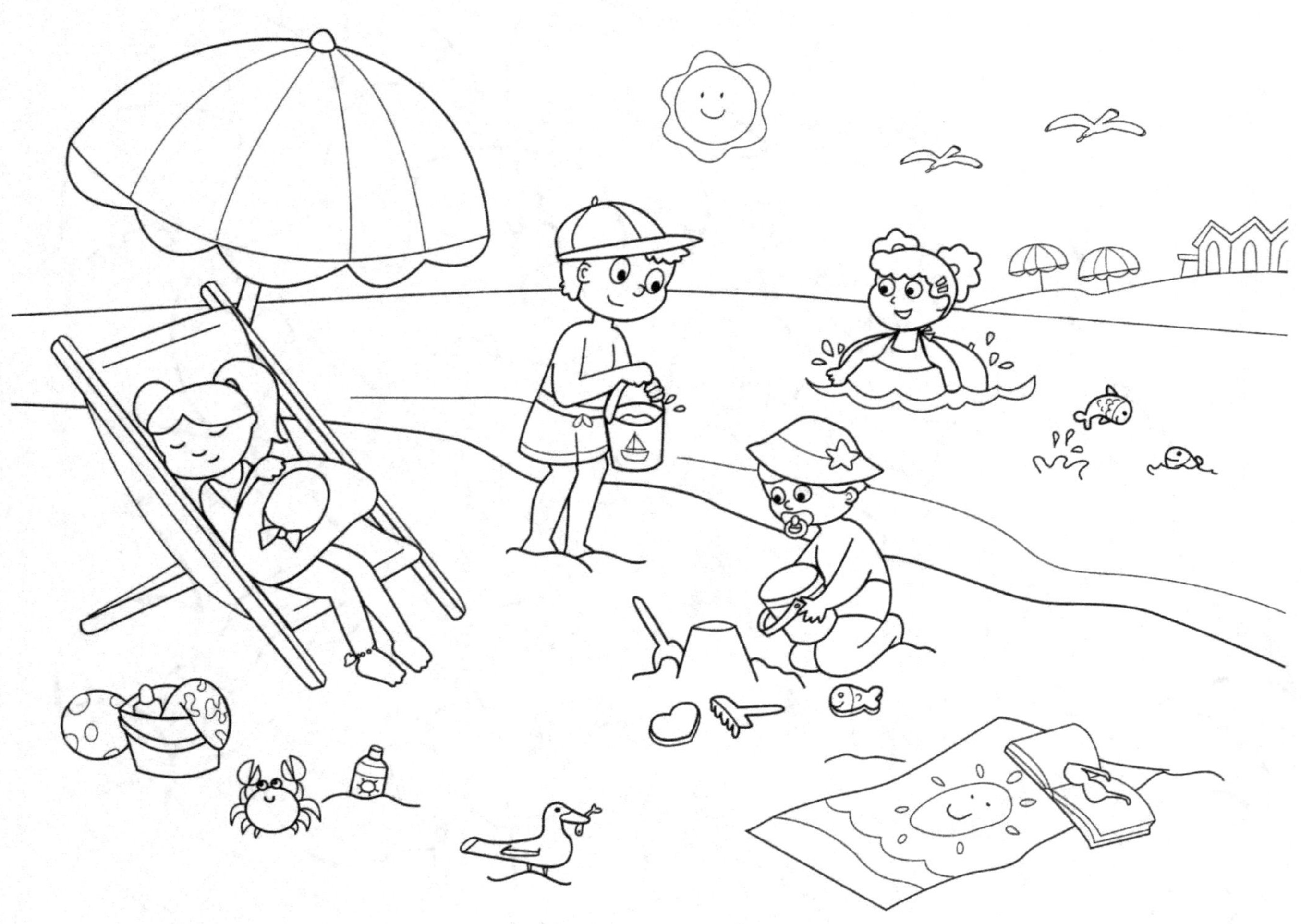

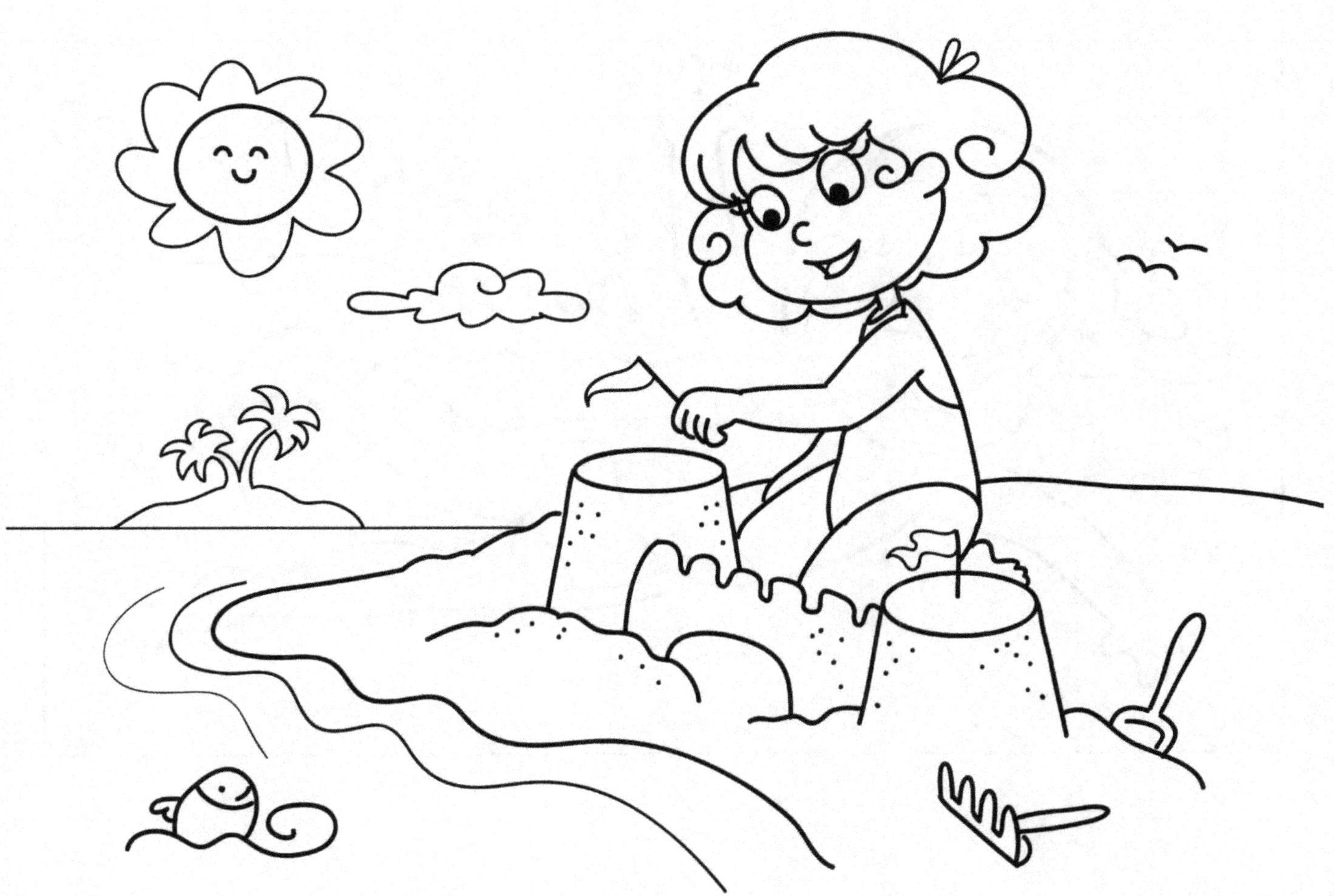

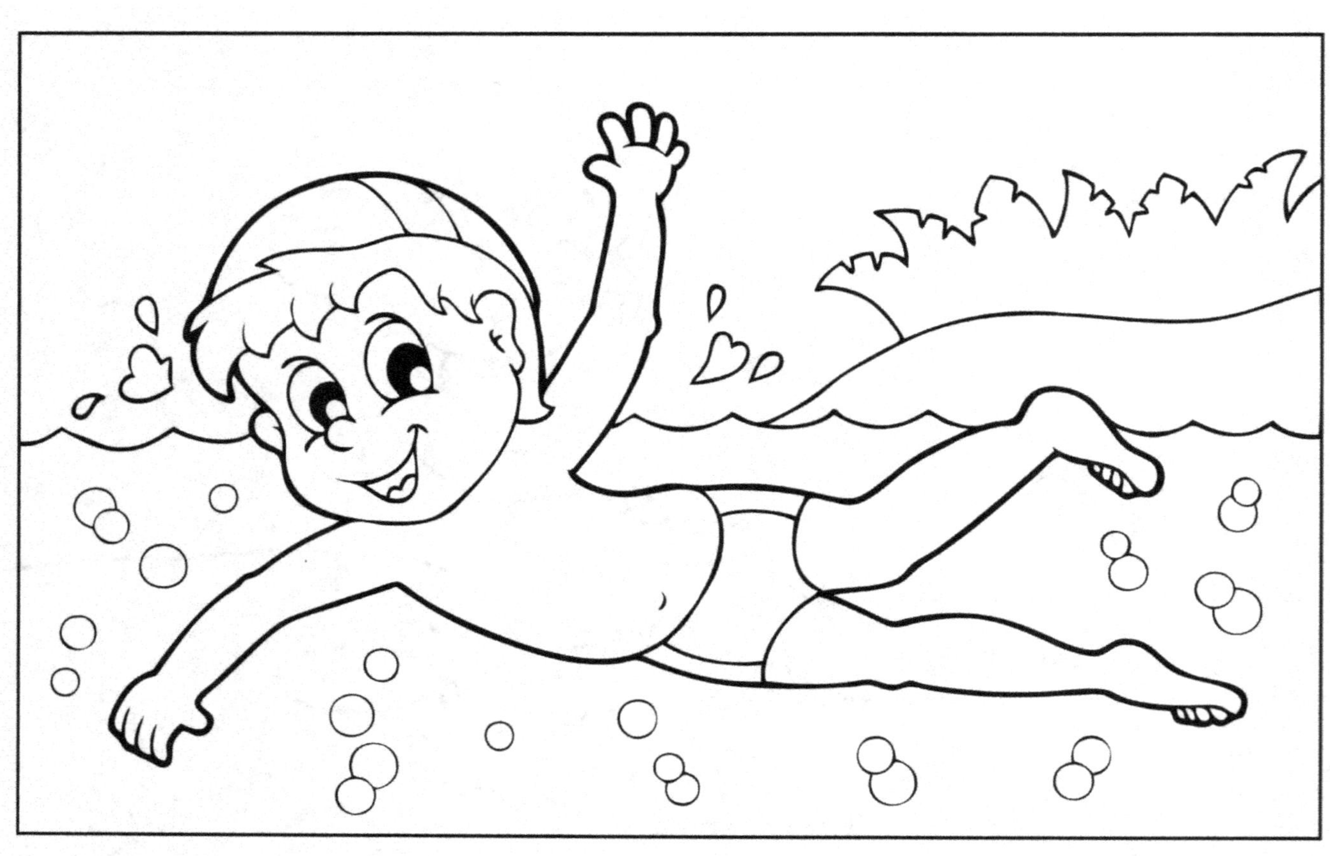

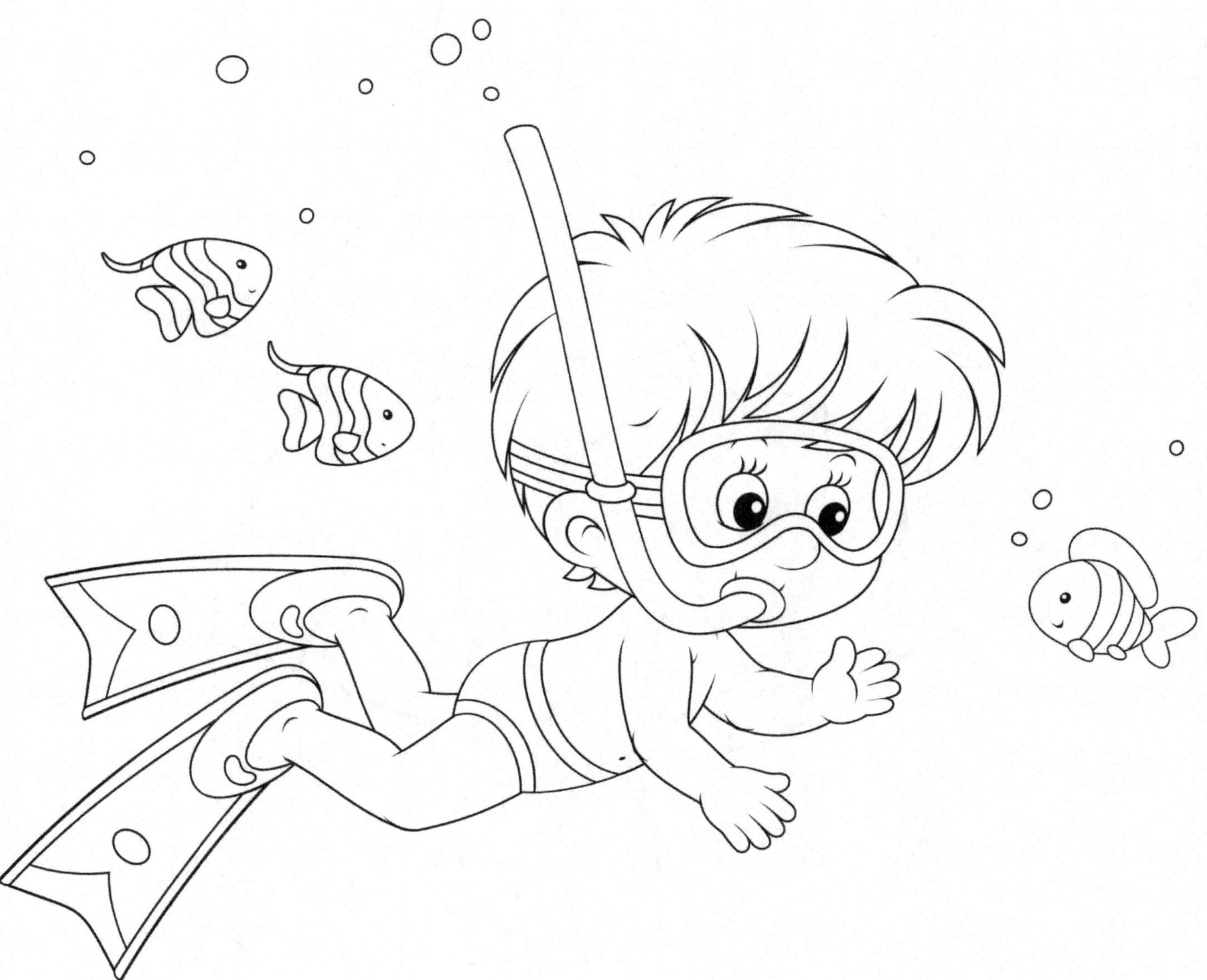

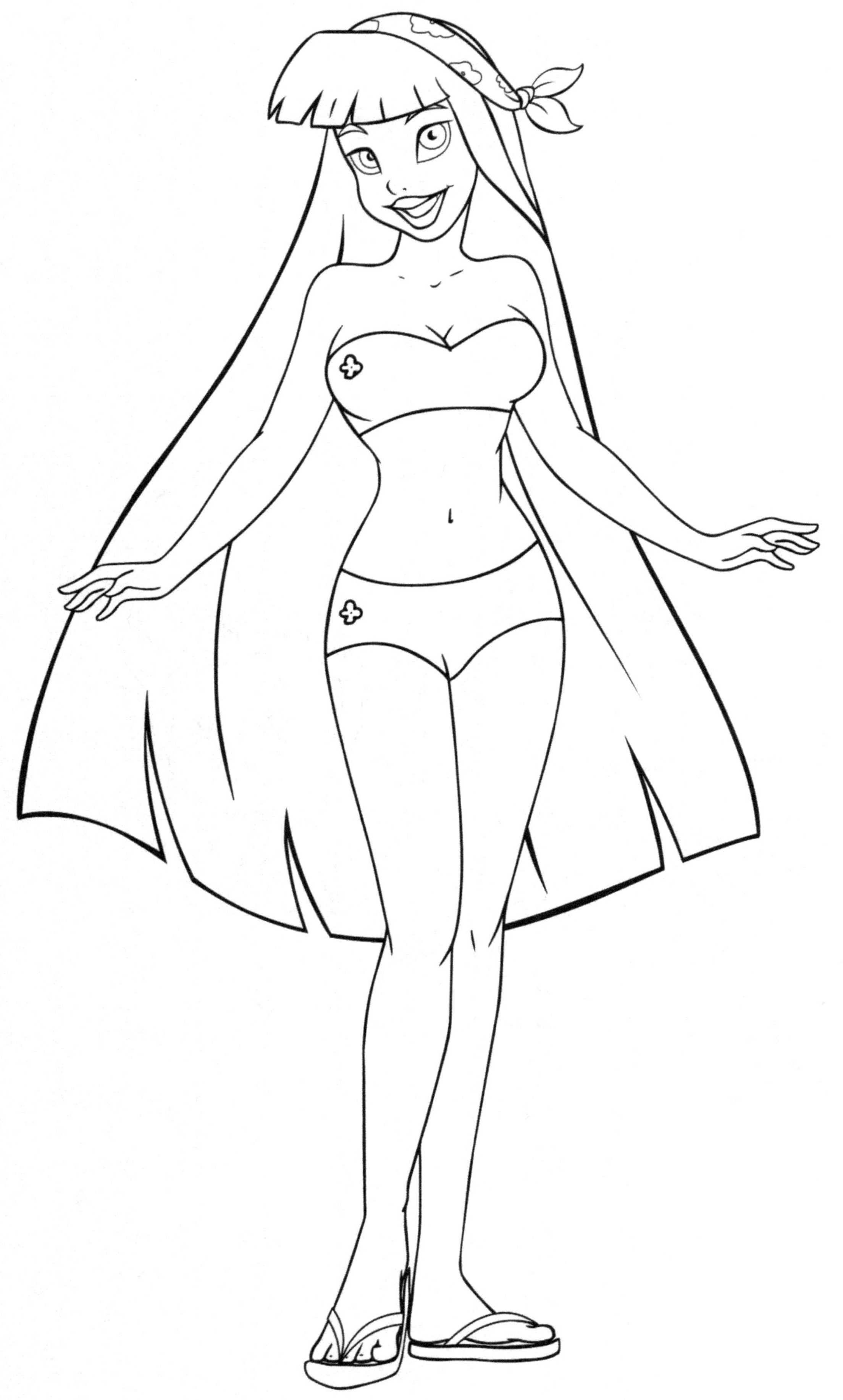

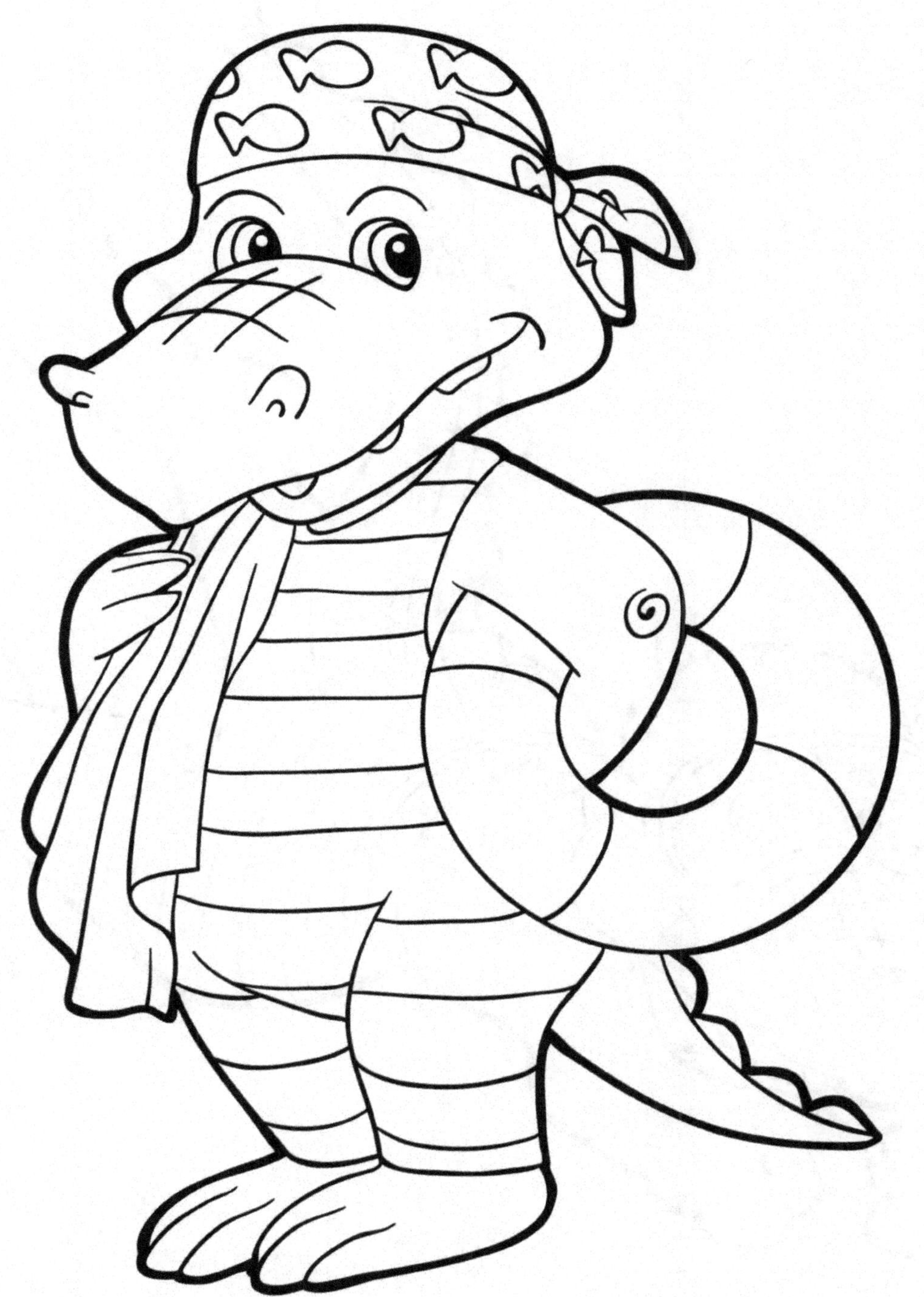

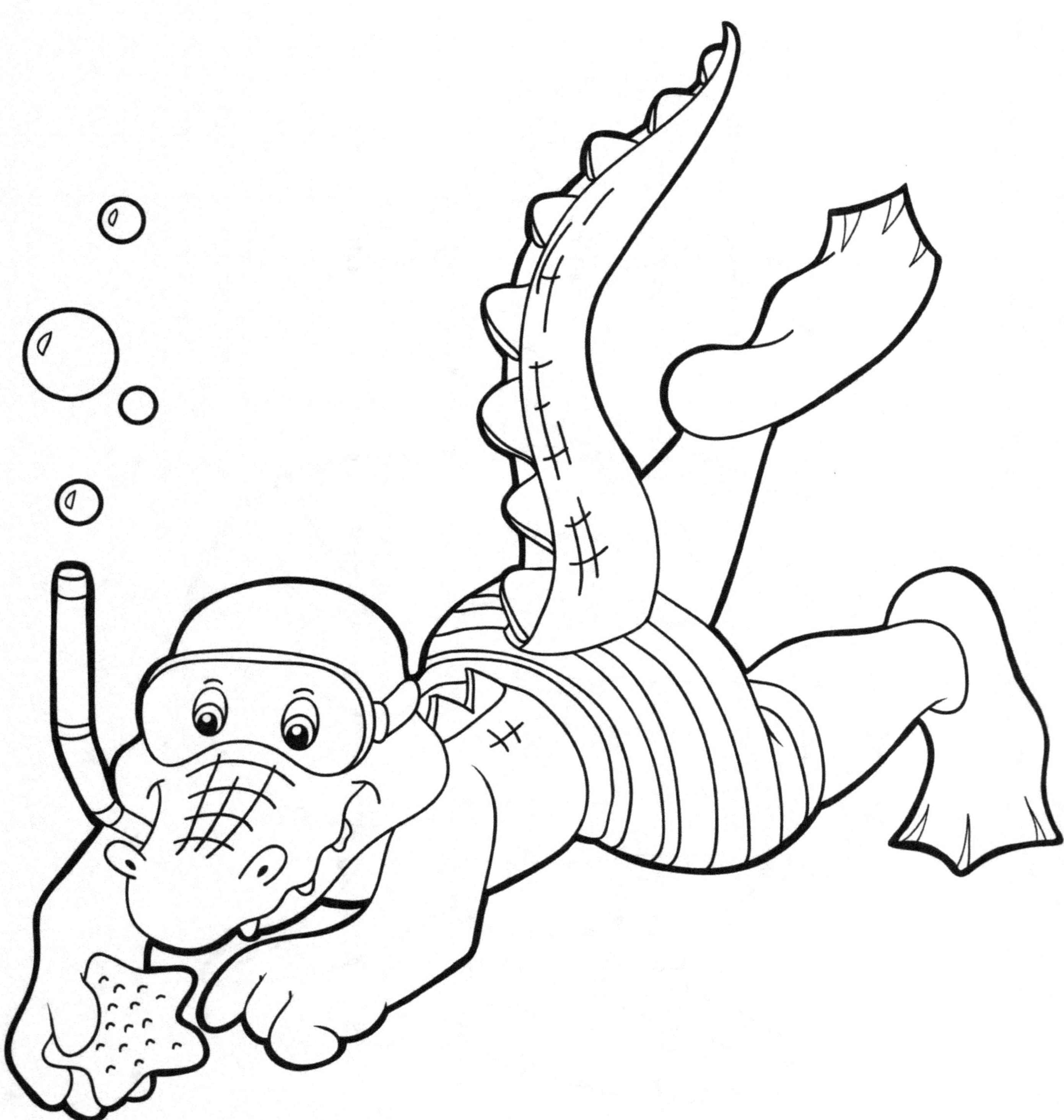

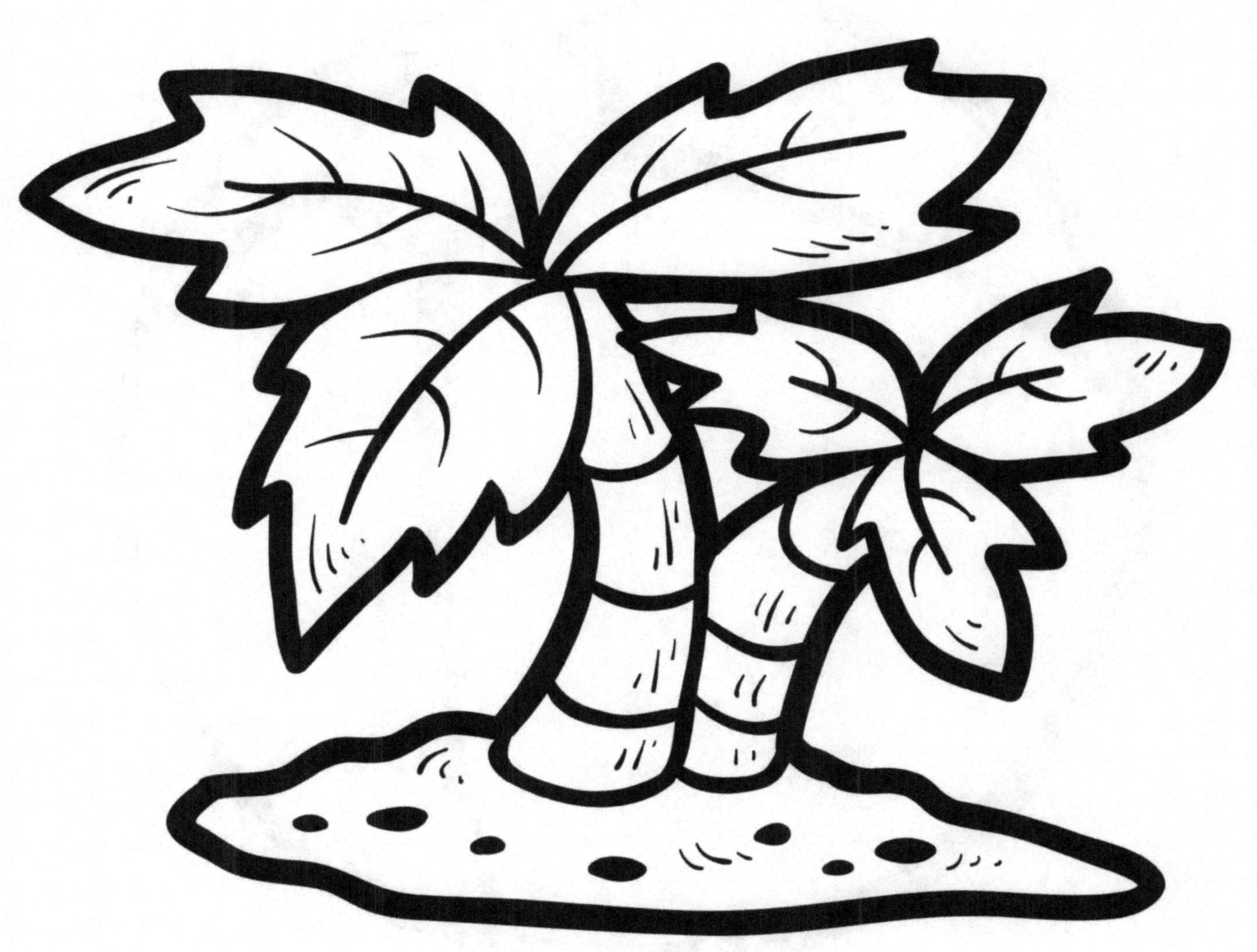

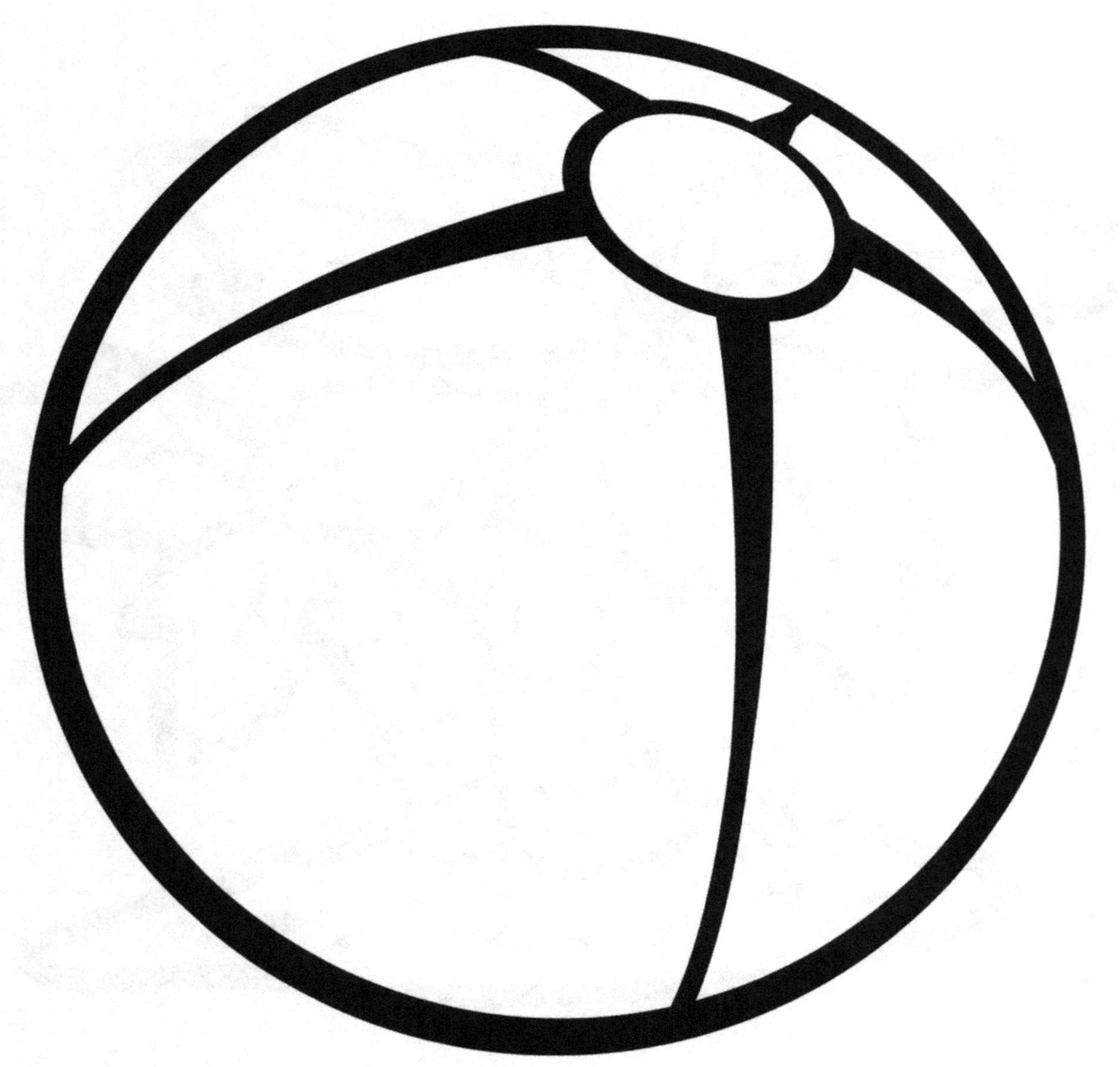

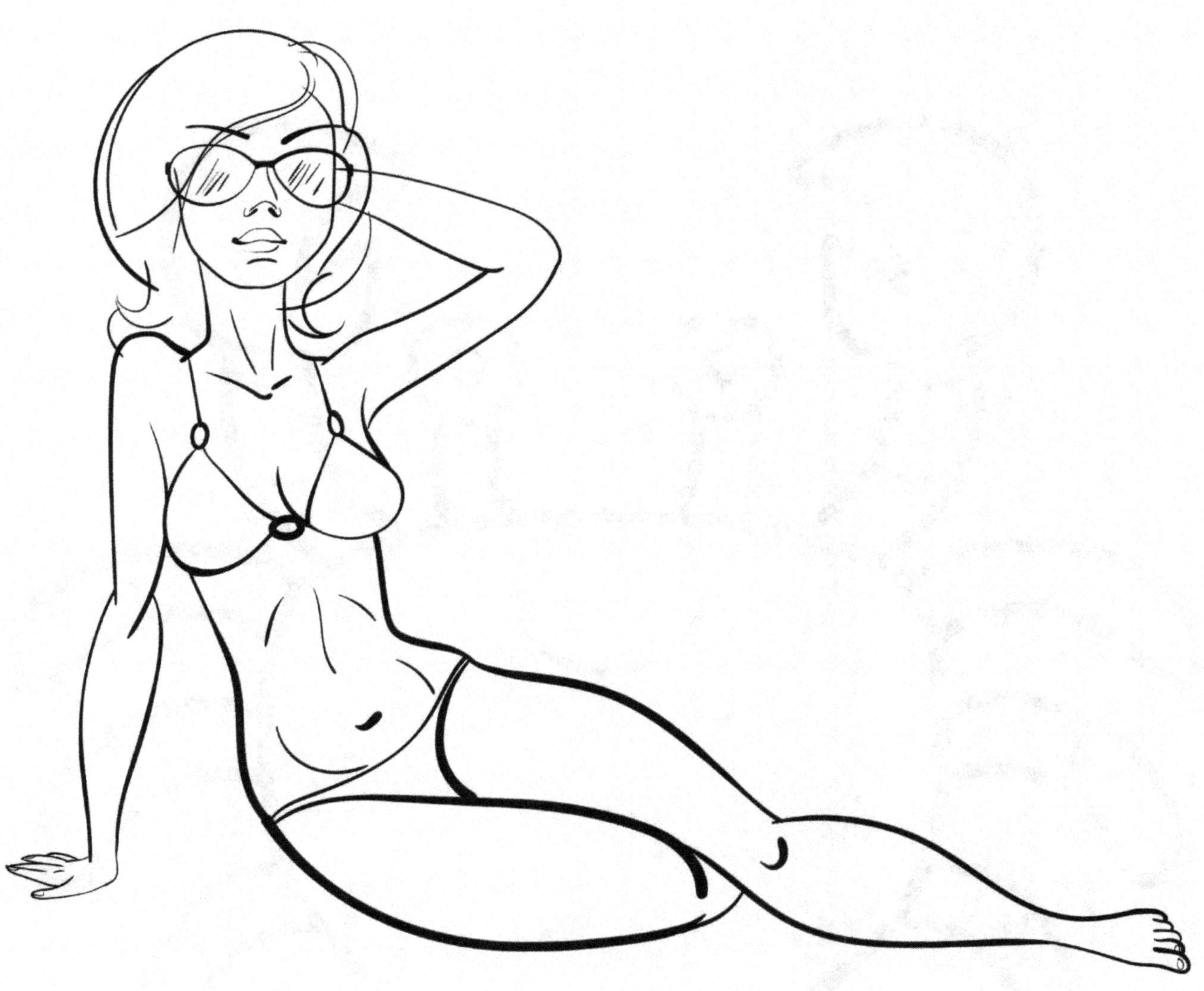

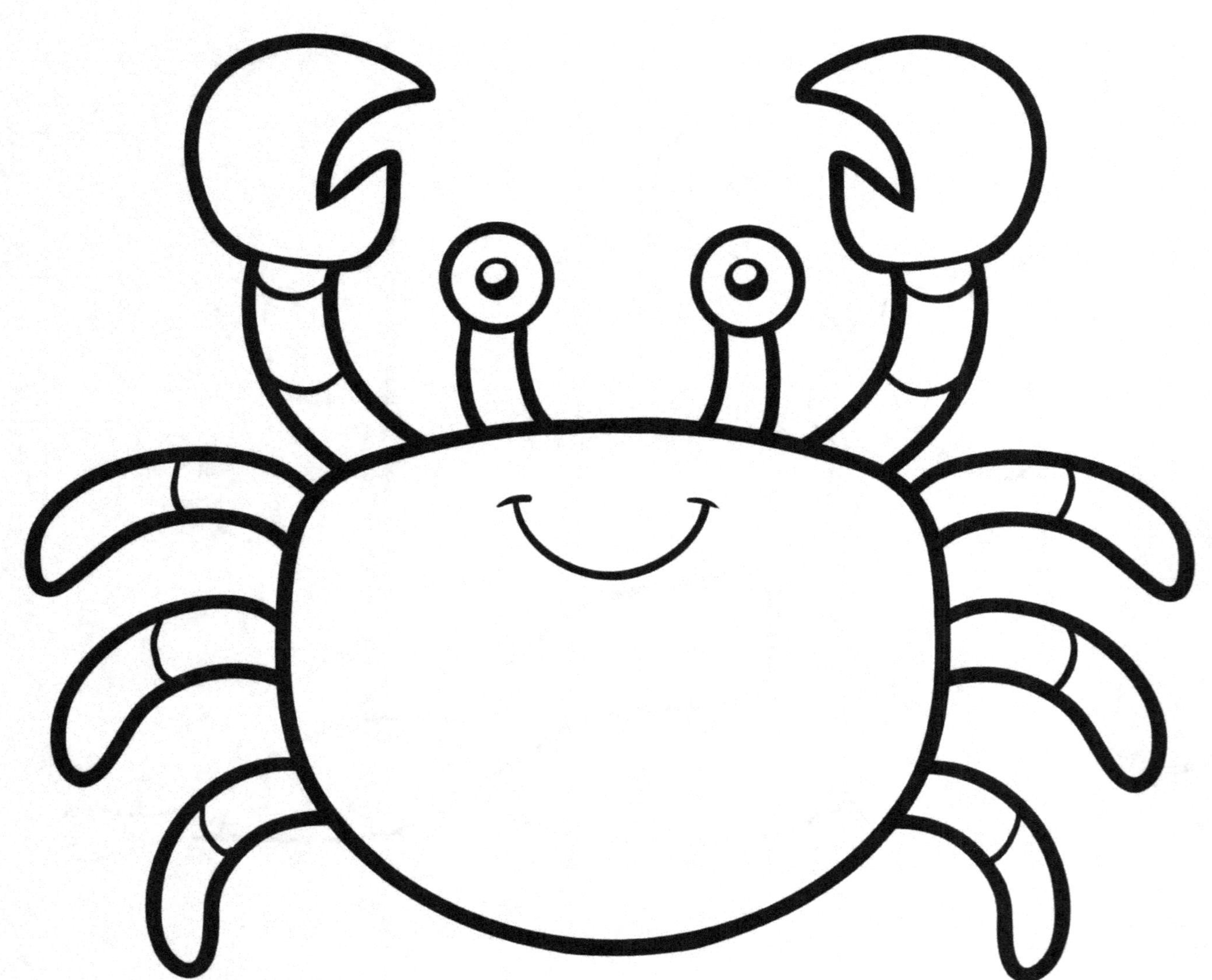

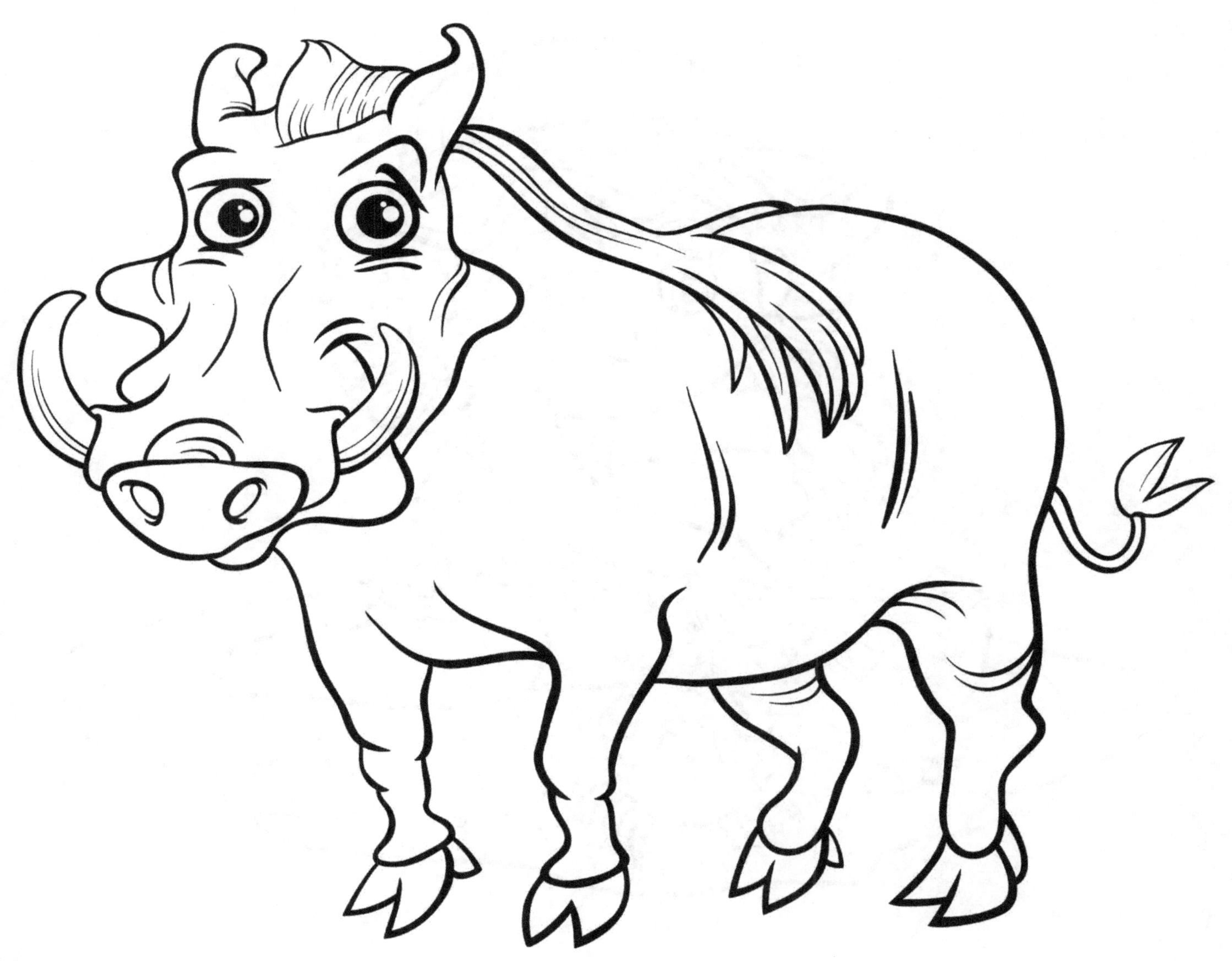

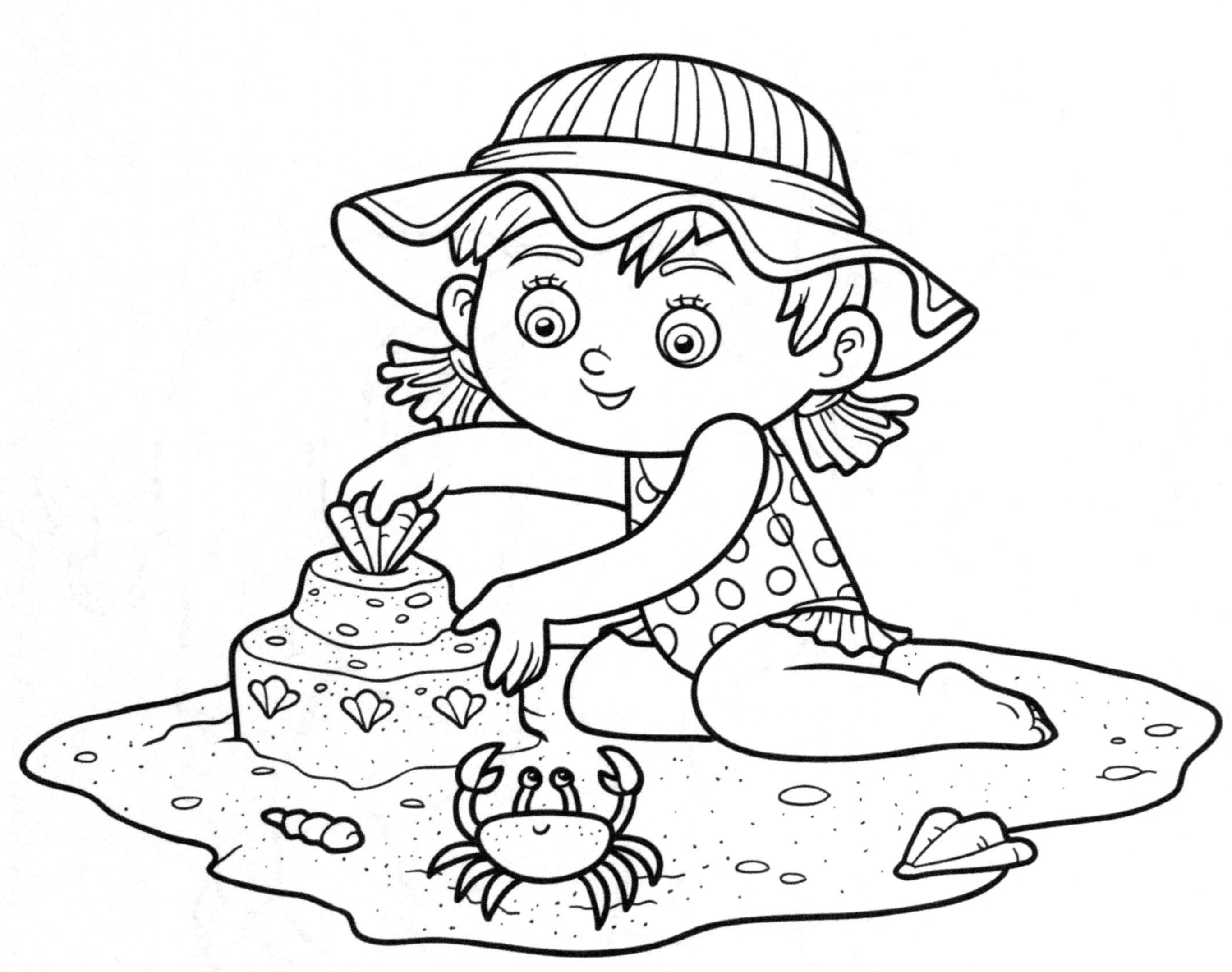

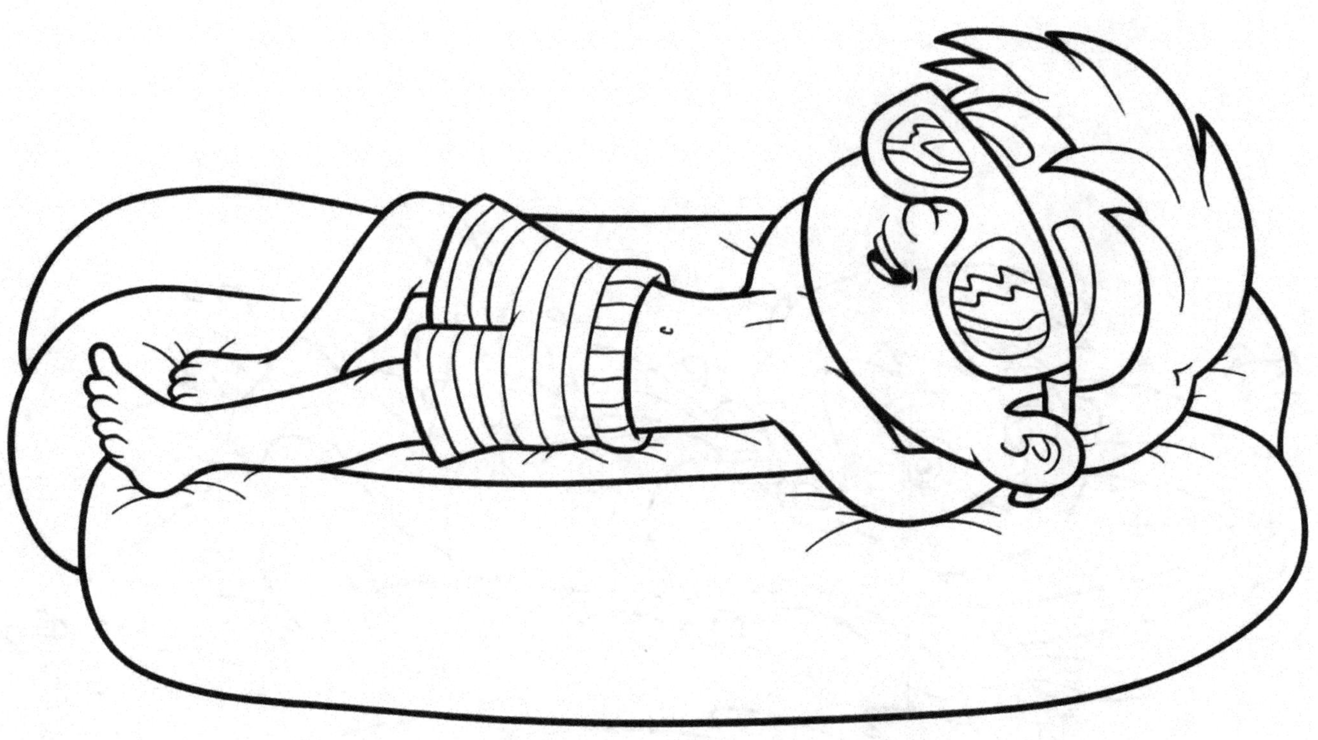

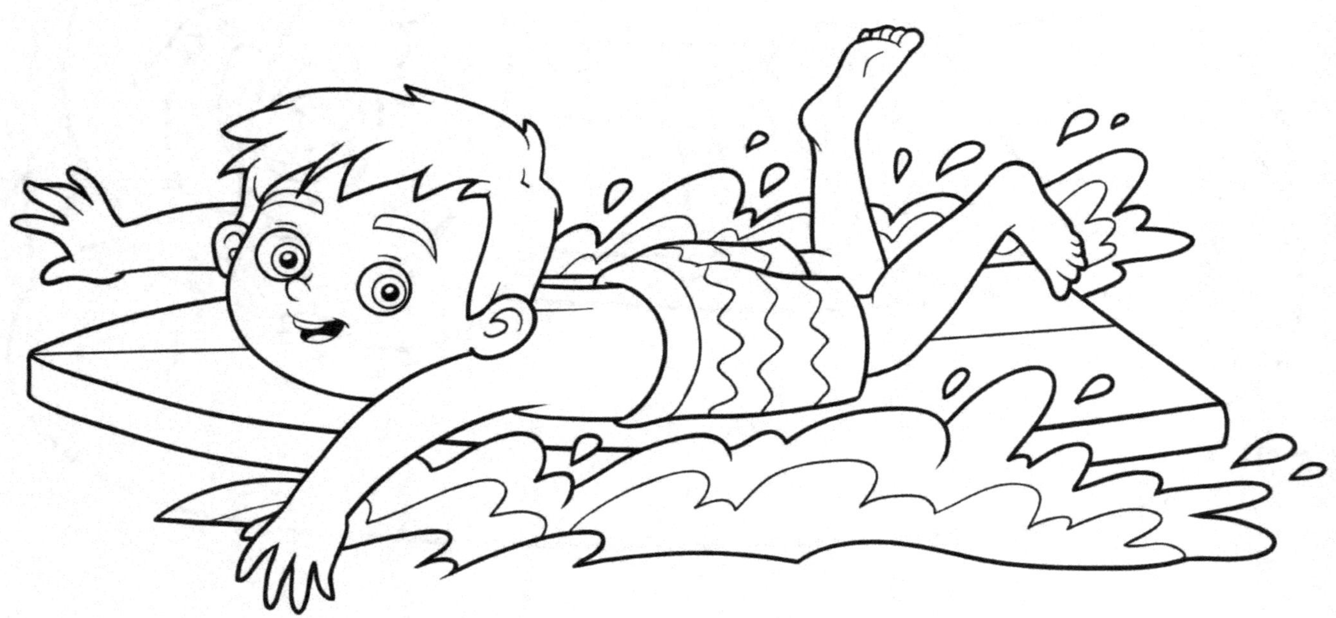

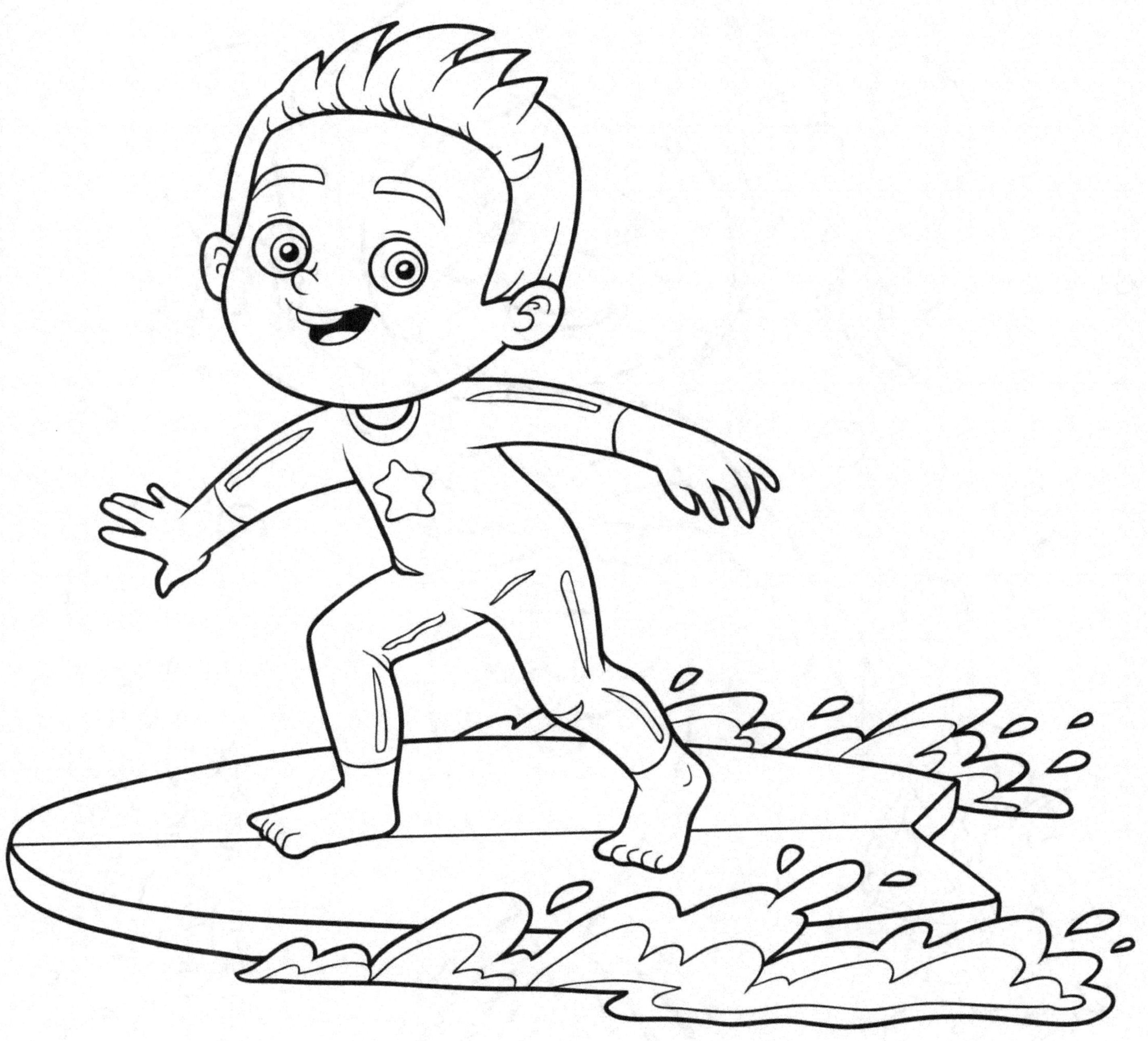

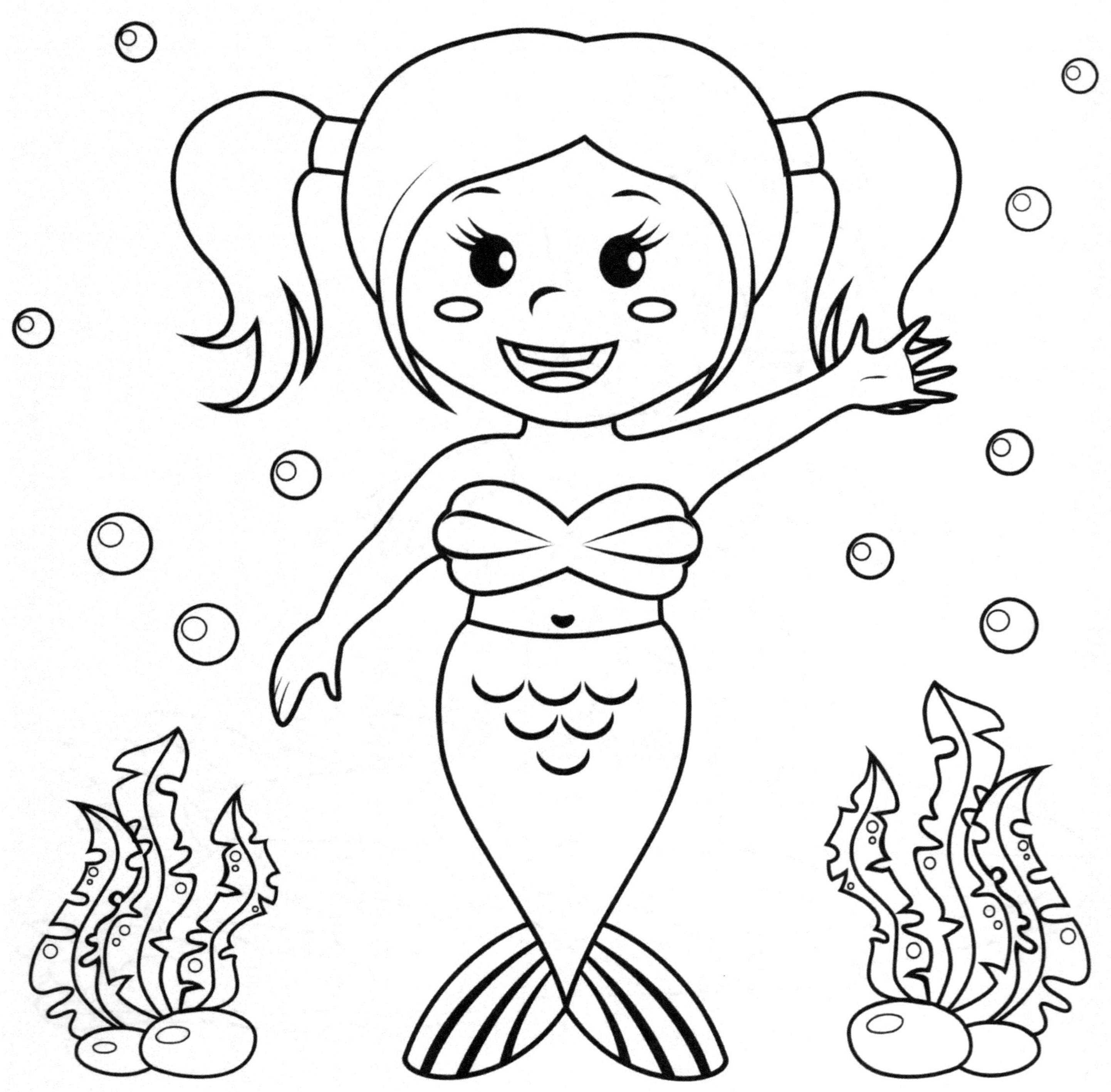